'Mammals' is a term  class of animal.

Mammals share va of animals; for insta have backbones and blooded. The features distinguish a mammal are as follows; it has a skin which is covered with hair (except in the case of some whales); it produces milk to feed its young; it has four limbs, except in the case of whales and dolphins. The limbs (as with seals) may be so adapted to a particular mode of life as to be hardly recognisable as such.

Zoologists divide mammals into nineteen 'orders', which are then divided into 'sub-orders' and again into 'families'. 'Families' can be divided into 'sub-families', but broadly speaking after 'families' the next most useful grouping is that of 'genus'. Finally, the different members of a 'genus' are divided into 'species', and sometimes into 'sub-species' or 'races' of a 'species'. These various groupings are given Latin names so that they may be scientifically and accurately identified all over the world.

For the purpose of this book we mostly use the following groupings: orders - families - species.

Notice that the mammals of Africa do not include Bears, Wolves or Deer (except for one very rare species.) Africa is the home of the great majority of Antelopes, and Madagascar the home of all the Lemurs in the world. Many species in Africa are in grave danger of extinction, and we should do all that we can to preserve them.

B I A

MALIA

AGASCAR

CEAN

1000

1600

A Ladybird Book
Series 691

'*African Mammals*' *is the first of a Ladybird series of books illustrating and describing animals of the world. Superb, full-colour illustrations have been specially prepared by John Leigh-Pemberton, the well-known bird and animal painter. These illustrations are supported by an informative text, and a coloured end-paper shows the various types of habitat of the animals. An index is given and also, at the back, a chart showing the various Orders and Families to which the animals belong.*

AFRICAN
MAMMALS

by
JOHN LEIGH-PEMBERTON

Publishers: Wills & Hepworth Ltd., Loughborough
First published 1969 © *Printed in England*

Galago (*above*)	Length, head and body 11·5–38 cm.
	Length of tail 15–40 cm.
Potto (*below*)	Length, head and body 32–39 cm.
	Length of tail 5–10 cm.

Both these animals belong to the order known as Primates (the same as that of humans), and to the family known as *Lorisidae*. They are nocturnal (as is indicated by their huge eyes), and inhabit the trees of dense forests. Both produce one or, at the most, three young per litter.

There are six species of Galago or Bush Baby; one of these, the Moholi Galago, is found more in bush country than in forest, and is the species most often kept as a pet. Galagos are extremely agile and capable of spectacular leaps. Their diet consists of grasshoppers, birds' eggs, fruit and flowers, and they make their homes in birds' old nests. A curious feature is their large ears which they can roll up either singly or together and either backwards or forwards.

Pottos, like Galagos, have the ends of their fingers and toes flattened, and are able to grip with finger and thumb. They use their hands cleverly and in a very human fashion for feeding, climbing and defence. Pottos make no nest but live in holes in trees, carrying their young about with them. They are very slow-moving but can grab quickly for food, which consists principally of insects, snails and fruit. The Potto's neck bones protrude as spines along the back of the neck, and when threatened the animal rolls up and presents these spines to the attacker.

Both animals utter loud cries, that of the Galago being rather bird-like.

7214 0236 4

Mangabey (*above*)

Length, head and body	35–85 cm.
Length of tail	45–75 cm.

Colobus (*below*)

Length, head and body	50–70 cm.
Length of tail	65–85 cm.

Both these Primates are forest dwellers—members of the family *Cercopithecidae*. However, the term 'Old World Monkeys' is perhaps easier to remember.

The four species of Mangabeys differ mainly in the colour and pattern of their fur, and all have pale eye-lids which they use when communicating with one another. Their long tails are used as aids to climbing but are not really suitable for grasping. Mangabeys eat fruit, leaves and nuts and some animal food. They have cheek pouches in which food is stored.

These quiet, shy but active monkeys live either in family groups or in larger bands of up to fifty members. They are found in the equatorial forests of Africa, from Liberia across the continent to Uganda and as far south as Angola.

Colobus Monkeys belong to what is known as the 'leaf-eating' branch of the family of Old World Monkeys. They very rarely leave the trees and, in spite of their size, are remarkably active in the tree-tops. They are entirely vegetarian and have no cheek pouches, but they have a digestive system specially adapted to the diet of leaves. The beautiful fur of the three species of Colobus has for centuries caused them to be hunted, and some of them are becoming rare, but apart from Man—and the Leopard—they have few enemies. They utter a characteristic bark when frightened.

Colobus range through the forest belt of Central Africa from the west coast to Abyssinia and, like Mangabeys, they are most active in the daytime. They seldom produce more than one offspring at a time.

Gorilla

Height (standing)	180 cm.
Arm span	250 cm.
Chest	175 cm.
Weight	200 kg.

The Gorilla is the largest, most powerful member of the order of Primates, and belongs to the family *Pongidae*. There is one species only, found in two forms—the Lowland Gorilla of the Cameroons and Congo River basin, and the Mountain Gorilla, which lives in isolated groups in the Eastern Congo and among the extinct volcanoes of the Great Rift Valley. The Mountain Gorilla, which is becoming rare, has longer hair and, in old males, a more pronounced crest on the back of the head.

Gorillas are diurnal (active in the daytime) and entirely vegetarian. They live peaceable lives in well-organised groups usually dominated by an old male, and tend to wander over a fairly wide area. At night the females and young of varying groups construct nests in the forks of trees, securing them with branches tied in recognisable knots, while the heavier males sleep at the foot of the trees. Gorillas normally walk on all fours, treading on the outer edges of the feet and on the knuckles of their partially closed hands. However, they can walk upright and will do so, particularly when angry or nervous. In this state a male Gorilla is a very formidable animal, possessing incredible strength and great courage and intelligence.

Gorillas produce one infant at a birth, and probably live for as long as fifty years. They make full use of their hands, are able to distinguish colours, and can communicate quite elaborately with one another by gesture, grimace and voice.

Chimpanzee

Height (standing)	150 cm.
Arm span	225 cm.
Weight (Males)	55–85 kg.
Weight (Females)	45–65 kg.

There are two species of Chimpanzee; the common species lives in tropical forests north of the Congo River, and the rare pygmy species (or Bonobo) lives to the south of the Congo River. The latter is much smaller, darker skinned and lighter built, and little is known about it. Both belong to the order of Primates and the family *Pongidae*.

In character Chimpanzees are quite different from Gorillas. They are excitable, inquisitive and arrogant, whereas the Gorilla is placid, stolid and retiring. Chimpanzees have a much more varied diet for, as well as nuts and fruits, they eat insects and hunt, kill and eat small mammals such as pigs or monkeys. They are very intelligent and it has recently been discovered that they employ instruments (such as a suitable twig) to extract grubs from holes in wood. They live in nomadic, mixed groups, mainly on the ground, but climb into trees more often than Gorillas. They sleep in roughly-made tree-nests at night, normally using them for one occasion only. They communicate by grimace and gesture, and make a very wide range of significant sounds.

Individual Chimpanzees vary enormously; some have pale faces, some black; some are very hairy and others almost bald. Generally speaking, and because of their excitable temperament and great strength, Chimpanzees are more dangerous in the wild state than Gorillas. They are said to live for about forty years, and normally produce a single infant at a birth, although twins are not unknown.

Ruffed Lemur

| Length, head and body | 45 cm. |
| Length of tail | 50 cm. |

On the island of Madagascar, and nowhere else in the world, are found the sixteen species of Lemur, Primates which belong to the family *Lemuridae*. They range in size from the minute Lesser Mouse Lemur (which is the smallest of all Primates) to the cat-sized Ruffed Lemur shown here. The larger species are active during the day, but most of the smaller Lemurs are nocturnal.

With the exception of the Ring-tailed Lemur, which lives among rocks, Lemurs are forest dwellers. They feed principally on fruit and insects but also take birds and honey. They are extremely agile and, propelled by their enormously developed hind legs, make tremendous leaps from tree to tree. When on the ground, some species walk upright. Lemurs produce one or two young at a birth, but Dwarf Lemurs usually produce triplets. Like many other Primates they live in well-organised social groups.

The Ruffed Lemur, which is becoming rare, is very variable in pattern and colouration and can be black and white or even black and russet. Like all Lemurs, it is equipped with padded fingers and powerful thumbs used for feeding and climbing, and a long tail extensively used for balancing. This is the only large Lemur known to make a nest.

Some Lemurs were once regarded as sacred by the natives of Madagascar, and so were not persecuted. Now, many species of this delightful animal are facing extinction due to the destruction, for agricultural purposes, of their forest habitat.

Okapi (*above*)

Shoulder height	250 cm.
Length, head and body	200 cm.
Length of tail	40 cm.

Duiker (*below*)

Shoulder height	40 cm.
Length, head and body	70 cm.
Length of tail	10 cm.

The order of *Artiodactyla* includes one hundred and ninety-four species. They are distinguished by an even number of toes on each foot and, among those species known as ruminants, possess a complicated digestive system which involves a special process known as 'chewing the cud'. The males of many species have antlers grown annually (in the case of deer), or horns (permanent in the case of antelopes and cattle). Both Okapis and Duikers belong to this order.

The Okapi, found in certain tropical forests of the Congo, was unknown until 1901. Okapis are timid, secretive animals, principally nocturnal, which live singly or in pairs and eat leaves and fruit. Males carry a pair of three-inch horns, and the tongue of an Okapi is so long that it can lick its own eyes. This is the only relative of the Giraffe, both belonging to the family Giraffidae. A single calf is born, oddly enough at the wettest season of the year.

The Duiker, a miniature antelope of the family Bovidae, is found throughout Africa south of the Sudan. There are seventeen species, some inhabiting the grasslands, while others live in the dense vegetation of the forest. Both sexes have little horns. Their diet is grass or leaves, according to habitat. A single offspring is produced at a birth, and the life span is said to be about eight years. Duikers are one of the principal food sources for many predators and are adept at diving for cover—hence the name 'Duiker', which means 'diving buck'.

Leopard

Shoulder height   ᴄ.
Length, head and body   *125* ᴄ.
Length of tail   *95 cm.*

The Leopard is a member of the order *Carnivora* and of the cat family—the *Felidae*. The Leopard is found in more countries than any other member of the cat family, being found in Korea, China and Java, as well as India and throughout most of Africa. It can stand extremes of climatic conditions and is at home in varying types of habitat, from dense jungle to mountain and grassland. Black Leopards are not a separate species, being merely what is known as a 'melanistic' (abnormally dark) form of the ordinary spotted type. These Black Leopards are commonest in India. Leopards have five toes on each fore-foot and four on each hind-foot, all with retractable claws. The name 'Panther' refers to the same animal.

In Africa the Leopard is principally a forest animal, preferring trees in which it waits for its prey, and to which it will often carry a carcass. This extremely powerful animal will kill anything from antelope and zebra to monkeys and dogs (to which it seems to be particularly addicted). It kills by biting through the neck or throat. Leopards are chiefly nocturnal, hiding during the day in thick cover. They are usually silent animals but with a distinctive cough, and they roar less than lions. From one to six (usually three) cubs are born at a birth, all blind and helpless. The life span is up to thirty years.

Leopards are good swimmers and, like other cats, can catch fish in shallow water. They are perhaps the most dangerous of all the big cats.

16

Serval

The order *Carnivora* is divided into seven families—the Dogs, Bears, Raccoons, Weasels, Genets, Hyaenas and Cats. The word 'carnivore' means 'flesh-eating', and generally this is true of all members of the order. There are, however, several exceptions, such as the vegetarian Giant Panda and the Aardwolf, a relative of the Hyaena, which lives almost entirely on termites (a kind of insect). Furthermore, this order now omits the Seals *(Pinnipedia)*—flesh-eating aquatic mammals, and the Shrews *(Insectivora)*, many of whom are carnivorous.

One of the most beautiful members of the cat family is the Serval, slender, elegant and found in two forms—the Large-spotted and the Small-spotted. Principally nocturnal, this animal is found in bush and forest country throughout Africa, south of the Sahara. It is never far from water and never found in deserts. It is a hunter of rodents and small antelope such as Duiker, but it is particularly successful at catching birds, either by climbing after them at roost or by catching them on the ground—or as they take off into the air. Over short distances it has remarkable speed.

The Serval's large ears indicate a greatly developed sense of hearing—so much so that it is said to be able to locate moles burrowing. Like other small cats it does not roar but has a repetitive yowling cry. Three kittens are born in a nest made in the abandoned burrow of some other animal, or in a thick clump of grass.

Anubis Baboon
(*above*)

| Length, head and body | 75 cm. |
| Length of tail | 50 cm. |

Springhare (*below*)

| Length, head and body | 40 cm. |
| Length of tail | 40 cm. |

Out in the grassland and bush, the principal representative of the Primates is the Baboon. Of these there are about seven species, belonging to the family of Old World Monkeys. This family includes the Drills and Mandrills (animals with strikingly-coloured skin areas on the face and which inhabit equatorial forests) and the Gelada Baboon, found in mountain ravines in Abyssinia. Baboons live in organised communities; they are omnivorous, eating roots and vegetables as well as grubs and small animals. They communicate by facial expression, gesture and voice, which in their case is a sharp bark. One young is born at a birth (very rarely more), and like all the higher Primates, Baboons are affectionate and devoted parents. They are aggressive animals with powerful jaws and formidable teeth; a group of Baboons is more than a match for their principal enemy, the Leopard.

The Springhare, or Springhaas, belongs to the family *Pedetidae* and the order *Rodentia*. Found in dry country in southern and eastern Africa, it is not really a hare at all. It is almost entirely nocturnal and lives on bulbs and roots, for which it digs with specially developed fore-feet. It travels at immense speed by means of a series of bounds (as much as nine metres) and is said to employ this leap on leaving its burrow in order to avoid lurking predators. One litter a year of one or two young are born in a chamber at the end of a complex burrow system.

Lion (*above*)

Length, head and body	*220 cm.*
Length of tail	*90 cm.*
Shoulder height	*75 cm.*

Lioness (*below*)

About 10 cm. smaller on all measurements.

In a genus *(Panthera)* by themselves are placed the so-called 'big cats' of the family *Felidae*.   These are the Lion, Tiger, Leopard, Jaguar and Snow Leopard. All have in common the ability to roar—not shared by the lesser members of the family who are, however, able to purr.

Lions were once found in Europe (up to A.D.100) and throughout India and the Middle East. Now, with the exception of a remnant in the Gir Forest in India, they chiefly inhabit central and eastern Africa south of the Sahara. There are still many thousands of Lions left but their future must be a matter for concern. Lions depend on the herds of Antelope and Zebra which form their staple diet, and if these diminish so does the number of Lions.

The Lion, which lives on the grassland and open plains is peculiar among cats in that it lives in groups or 'prides' consisting of from three to twenty members dominated by a mature male. A pride hunts co-operatively, the lionesses doing most of the killing—usually by a blow from a massive fore-paw and a bite through the throat. A pride of four Lions kills one sizeable animal a week. They are mainly nocturnal, sleeping for as much as nineteen hours a day. Unlike other cats, they often sleep in the open.

About four spotted cubs are born in a den. There is a high infant mortality rate, but once grown, a Lion may live for as long as twenty years.

Vervet Monkey
(above)

Cheetah *(below)*

Length, head and body	50 cm.
Length of tail	75 cm.
Length, head and body	145 cm.
Length of tail	75 cm.
Shoulder height	100 cm.

The graceful little Vervet Monkey is a form of the very common species of Grass Monkey (genus *Cercopithecus*), found throughout Africa south of the Sahara, in country which has both grass and trees. It is a member of the large family of Old World Monkeys and lives in groups, sometimes of mixed species, which can be a great menace to crops.

The diet is mainly vegetarian, but also includes young birds, reptiles and insects. Vervets are equally at home on the ground or in trees, and they are good swimmers. One infant at a birth is usual.

The Cheetah differs in many respects from the other cats, and is placed in a separate genus *(Acinonyx)* by itself. Its claws do not retract fully and its feet are more like those of a dog, as indeed are many of its habits. This is an animal of the grasslands. It needs both thick bush for protection and the open plain for hunting. Mainly diurnal, Cheetahs hunt by a preliminary stalk followed by a final dash at enormous speed. Up to a distance of 5,000 metres it is the fastest land animal in the world. It is the most tameable of the cats and has for centuries been used by man for coursing. Gazelles, hares and large birds provide most of its food.

When the two to four young are born, they are covered in a greyish, fluffy mane and have retractile claws, but the mane and retractability of the claws are lost at about two months. Cheetah cubs utter an unusual bird-like chirp.

Spotted Hyaena
(above)

Black-backed Jackal
(below)

Length, head and body	140 cm.
Length of tail	25 cm.
Shoulder height	80 cm.
Length, head and body	60 cm.
Length of tail	30 cm.

The three species of Hyaena are grouped together in their own family *(Hyaenidae)* among the *Carnivora,* and to them must be added their peculiar insectivorous relative, the Aardwolf.

The Spotted Hyaena is found throughout most of Africa south of the Sahara. It is normally nocturnal and solitary, and until recently was thought to live almost entirely on carrion (the remains of dead animals). It is now established that to a great extent Hyaenas kill their own food and, although reputed to be cowardly, a group of them will attack and kill even a Lion, if it is old or sick. They give out a terrible smell and their hideous howl finishes in a sort of mad laugh. Their teeth, jaws and necks are astonishingly powerful, and they can outrun a horse. Two young are born each year in a cave or burrow.

Jackals belong to the order *Carnivora,* family *Canidae,* the same as Dogs, and there are four species of them, all found in Africa. One of the species is found in India and Turkestan.

The Black-backed Jackal of the grasslands of eastern and southern Africa is a scavenger which relies partly for its living on the remains of kills left by Lions or other cats. These Jackals form packs which can hunt quite large animals. They are nocturnal, lying up by day in thickets, holes or, in very hot weather, in water. Two or more pups are born in a burrow; these join their parents in hunting or scavenging at eight weeks old.

African Elephant

Length, head and body	700 cm.
Length of tail	100 cm.
Shoulder height	350 cm.
Weight	5–7·5 metric tons

The order *Proboscidea* contains only one family *(Elephantidae)*, and two species, the African and Indian Elephant.

The African Elephant is the largest land mammal, the bull usually being larger than the cow. Both sexes have tusks, those of a mature bull being as much as 240 cm. in length. For centuries Elephants have been hunted, often illegally, for the ivory of their tusks.

In Africa, Elephants are found in tropical regions, sometimes on grassland but also in dense forest where they tend to be smaller. They need trees and plenty of water, which they can detect below ground and for which they will dig. The African Elephant differs from the Indian species in being larger and having much larger ears, a flat forehead, a concave back and usually only three toes as opposed to the Indian Elephant's four on the hind-foot.

Elephants live in wandering herds of mixed ages and sexes, and of which the leader can be either a bull or a cow. Their sense of mutual protection is very strong, and when nervous they are extremely dangerous. African Elephants are reputed to be untameable, but in fact are not hard to tame. Allied to their great strength is a remarkable intelligence. They have an unusual sensitivity of touch in the trunk and foot.

Elephants are vegetarian and live as long as seventy years. During her life a cow may have four or five calves; these are not fully weaned until two years old, and maturity is reached after about sixteen years.

Brindled Gnu (*above*)	*Length, head and body*	*180 cm.* .
	Length of tail	*40 cm.*
	Shoulder height	*130 cm.*
	Length of horns	*40 cm.*
Eland (*below*)	*Length, head and body*	*300 cm.*
	Length of tail	*40 cm.*
	Shoulder height	*170 cm.*
	Length of horns	*100 cm.*

The *Bovidae,* the family of Cattle, Antelopes, Goats and Sheep, makes up by far the greater part of the order *Artiodactyla.* Of all the mammal families this is the one of most importance to man, and Africa is rich in the number of species to be found there. All *Bovidae* are either grazers (grass-eaters) or browsers (leaf-eaters).

The Gnu, or Wildebeest, is found in two species. One of these, the White-tailed, is practically extinct. The Brindled Gnu is common in herds of about thirty on the grasslands of eastern and southern Africa, and travels great distances in search of the water supplies which are essential to it. It is very wary, posting 'sentries' round the herd and, when threatened, performing curious, almost dance-like antics. The young, often born while the herd is on the move, are very vulnerable to predators such as Hyaenas.

There are also two species of Eland: the Common Eland of southern Africa, which lives in bush and grass country, and the Giant Eland of the Sudan and West Africa and which is a rare forest dweller.

The Common Eland is a heavy, ox-like Antelope which lives in small herds and is both a browser and grazer. It is not aggressive and can be domesticated. There are herds of this animal on farms not only in Africa but even in the Soviet Union in the Crimea. It can be used for pulling carts and ploughs, as well as for a source of food.

Elands are great jumpers but poor gallopers and can exist for long periods without water.

Giraffe (*above*)

Length, head and body	400 cm.
Height at shoulder	350 cm.
Head height	500 cm.

White Rhinoceros
(*below*)

Length, head and body	420 cm.
Height at shoulder	200 cm.
Weight	3·5 metric tons

The single species of Giraffe (family *Giraffidae*) has many forms which are found in bush and wooded country from south of the Sahara to the Cape. Because of their height, these animals are extremely successful browsers, able to reach foliage unattainable by any competitor. Although it is the tallest and longest-necked mammal, the Giraffe has the usual seven vertebrae in the neck. Its height, combined with exceptional eyesight, gives it the greatest range of vision of any mammal. It is well able to defend itself, even against Lions, by a most savage kick and by blows from the head, which has from two to five small horns. Giraffes have a single calf at each birth, and this stands at about 200 cm. high when born.

The Rhinoceros belongs to the order *Perissodactyla* (odd-toed ungulates—hoofed), which also contains the families of Horses *(Equidae)* and Tapirs *(Tapiridae)*. There are five species of Rhinoceros, two of them African, and all are threatened with extinction or are in urgent need of protection.

The 'White' Rhinoceros is not white but grey, the word 'white' being a corruption of the Afrikaans word 'weit', indicating the 'wide' mouth of this animal, which is a grazer.

Second only to the Elephant in size, the White Rhinoceros has been rescued from extinction by careful conservation and now exists in mixed grass and woodland in two separate areas—Uganda and Zululand. Poor eyesight but good senses of smell and hearing are characteristic of this species, which has few enemies except Man—although a Lion may take an occasional calf.

Impala (*top*)	Length, head and body	125 cm.
	Shoulder height	80 cm.
	Length of horns (av.)	65 cm.
Thomson's Gazelle	Length, head and body	100 cm.
(*centre*)	Shoulder height	62 cm.
	Length of horns (av.)	33 cm.
Wart Hog (*below*)	Length, head and body	105 cm.
	Shoulder height	76 cm.
	Length of tusks	35 cm.

Impala (family *Bovidae*) inhabit open woodland of southern and eastern Africa and are both browsers and grazers. Only the male has horns, but both sexes have a tuft of black hair related to a gland on the hind leg. A herd of Impala can number several hundreds and be led by an old male. For protection, herds associate with other species such as Zebra. Impala are spectacular jumpers—bounds of nine metres long and three metres high being frequent when in full flight. There is a single calf at each birth.

Thomson's Gazelle—'Tommie'—is one of the commonest animals of the grasslands of East Africa. These Gazelles form two kinds of small herds—females and an adult male, or herds of young males only. Typical is the constantly wagging tail and the tendency to mix with other Antelopes. Single fawns are born twice a year. Tommies migrate as much as a hundred miles to find water during the dry season. They are hunted principally by Cheetah.

The Wart Hog belongs to the family *Suidae* of the order *Artiodactyla,* and is one of four species of Hog found in Africa. It inhabits open woodland throughout most of Africa, is chiefly vegetarian and, in spite of a ferocious appearance, is inoffensive unless provoked.

Wart Hogs love water and, in particular mud in which they wallow. They live in holes which they always enter backwards, and are active in daylight. From two to four piglets are born in each litter. Wart Hogs are much hunted by Leopards. The purpose of the male's facial 'warts' is not really known.

Hartebeest (*above*)

Length, head and body	175 cm.
Shoulder height	130 cm.
Length of horns	35 cm.

Black Rhinoceros
(*below*)

Length, head and body	350 cm.
Length of tail	70 cm.
Shoulder height	145 cm.

The family *Bovidae* contains two species of Hartebeest and six species of their near relations, the Damalisks. All are fairly large Antelopes living in small herds on grassland from the Sudan to the Cape. Some races are dying out and only survive through protection. They are all tremendously fast gallopers, relying on speed for safety. In Africa the Hartebeest is second only to the Cheetah for speed.

These grazers have fine lyre-shaped horns, and the long face and low hindquarters are also characteristic. A single calf at a birth is usual. Their chief enemy is the Lion, and like many Antelopes they seek protection with herds of other species such as Wildebeest and Zebra, one type resting while the other feeds or watches.

The Black Rhinoceros is a smaller animal than the White, weighing as much as two metric tons less. Like all other Rhinos it has been ruthlessly hunted for its horn, which is mistakenly believed by some Eastern peoples to have miraculous medicinal properties. As a result, the once numerous Black Rhino is now becoming scarce.

This is a browsing animal which happily eats the most terrible thorns. It is more aggressive than the White Rhino, being quite prepared to charge a truck or even the smell or sound of one. A distinguishing feature is the pointed upper lip which is capable of grasping leaves. The front horn averages some 50 cm. in length, the rear horn being shorter.

The Black Rhino inhabits bush country from Lake Chad to the Cape.

Sable Antelope (*above*)	Length, head and body	200 cm.
	Length of tail	45 cm.
	Shoulder height	150 cm.
	Length of horns	100 cm.
Kudu (*centre*)	Length, head and body	235 cm.
	Length of tail	45 cm.
	Shoulder height	150 cm.
	Length of horns	110 cm.
Zebra (*below*)	Length, head and body	220 cm.
	Length of tail	50 cm.
	Shoulder height	130 cm.

Two handsome members of the family *Bovidae* are the Sable Antelope of East Africa (whose relative, the Giant Sable Antelope, lives under protection in Angola), and the Kudu, one of a group of nine spiral-horned Antelopes found in varying habitats from Abyssinia to the Cape.

Sable Antelopes range from Kenya to the Transvaal, usually in light forest areas. These grazers associate with Zebra and Kudu in small herds composed of cows with one bull, or in smaller groups of bulls. The splendid horns (much larger in the Giant Sable) are borne by both sexes and can deal with all enemies, including Lions. The single calf is born with a red coat.

Rarely seen, the bull Kudu is a shy animal which hides by day in cover. The more evident cows are smaller and without horns. These somewhat solitary browsers form small herds only to breed. Kudu are found in wooded hills from Abyssinia to the Cape. They have the loudest bellow of any Antelope.

There are three species of Zebra (family *Equidae*), one of which, the Mountain Zebra, exists in two races—both rare and protected—in Cape Province.

The Zebras of the plains and mountains of eastern and central Africa are also of various races, differentiated chiefly by the pattern of their stripes.

Zebras feed at night but can be seen during the day, and are among the commonest African animals. They live in herds and are grazers, producing one foal at a birth. They form the chief food source for Lions.

Cape Buffalo (*above*)

Length, head and body	250 cm.
Shoulder height	130 cm.
Weight, up to	800 kg.

Hunting Dog (*below*)

Length, head and body	90 cm.
Length of tail	35 cm.
Shoulder height	60 cm.

These two animals are perhaps the most dangerous in Africa, both having considerable intelligence and stamina, combined with a markedly savage disposition.

The Cape Buffalo (family *Bovidae*) of South and East Africa was once very numerous, but has declined greatly in recent years, partly through the incidence of rinderpest—a disease affecting hoofed animals—and partly through hunting. Herds of a thousand or so still exist in the reserves wherever there is thick bush with some tree canopy (for shelter during the day) and a water supply for wallowing in as well as for drinking.

Buffaloes are grazers and browsers. They produce one calf at each birth, usually in January. This animal attacks whether it is provoked or not. It stalks an adversary or waits in ambush for him; a charge is followed by tossing, goring and finally kneeling on the victim. A dwarf race exists in the forests of central and western Africa.

The African Hunting Dog, taking the place in Africa of Wolves elsewhere, is a member of the family *Canidae*. It inhabits most of East Africa except for deep forest and is active by day and night.

This animal hunts in organised packs of up to sixty, running down its prey in relays until it is exhausted. It kills more than it can eat and Antelopes fear it more than they do a Lion. Only the biggest animals such as Buffalo are immune from attack.

Six to eight pups are produced at one birth at varying times of the year.

Hippopotamus
(above)

Length, head and body	*400 cm.*
Shoulder height	*150 cm.*
Weight	*3–4·5 metric tons*

Waterbuck *(below)*

Length, head and body	*200 cm.*
Shoulder height	*130 cm.*
Length of horns	*92 cm.*

The family *Hippopotamidae* contains only two species, the Hippopotamus and the Pygmy Hippopotamus. Mainly aquatic vegetarians, both produce a single, very small calf at each birth, but differ in many other respects.

The Hippopotamus, found in rivers and lakes from the Nile (Sudan) to the Orange River (Cape), is most abundant in central Africa. It feeds at night, mostly on grass, and sleeps by day among reeds or in deep pools, only the eyes and nostrils being above water. Hippos can stay totally submerged for more than five minutes and can walk about on the river bottom. Usually placid, a nervous Hippo will attack and capsize a boat. The males tend to fight each other savagely, using their gigantic teeth.

Calves are born and suckled under water and are vulnerable to attack from crocodiles.

The Pygmy Hippo of West Africa is more pig-like in behaviour and is a forest animal.

The Waterbucks, Lechwe, Kobs and Reedbucks form a tribe of Antelopes which never move far from water, and which are somewhat deer-like in behaviour. Coarse-haired and with fine horns, they are found in marsh or reed-beds and sometimes in woodland throughout the continent from south of the Sahara and the Nile Valley.

Waterbucks, which have the longest horns, are graceful and fast, and the slightly smaller Lechwe is a great swimmer, often feeding on aquatic plants. The Kob and Reedbuck are smaller still. In tropical forests the tribe is replaced by the Marshbuck or Sitatunga, a relative of the Kudu.

Arabian Camel

The family *Camelidae* contains six species, one in Africa, one in Asia and four in South America. All have in common a long neck, small head and a cleft upper lip, and all but two species have been domesticated.

There are no truly wild Arabian Camels left in the world today. It is probable that they have been domesticated animals for at least three thousand years, and used as beasts of burden, for riding, for food, hair and milk. They are perfectly adapted for desert life and able to go for long periods without water, although this is essential for their health. They are capable of storing food in the fatty, single hump, are equipped with two-toed, padded feet ideal for walking in sand or snow, and are almost impervious to heat or cold. They can (and do) eat anything vegetable and will drink even salt water. They have a double row of eyelashes and can close their nostrils completely.

Arabian Camels are found not only in the desert areas of Africa. Exported all over the world as working animals, they can be seen in the United States, India and Australia.

They are notably bad-tempered and have a savage bite. In spite of so many centuries of domestication, they still remain aloof from Man. Selective breeding has achieved various refinements—notably the Dromedary, a slender long-legged animal specially bred for riding and racing.

A single calf, mature in five years, is produced at a birth every other year.

Fennec Fox (*above*)

Length, head and body	40 cm.
Length of tail	30 cm.
Length of ears	15 cm.

Jerboa (*below*)

Length, head and body	14 cm.
Length of tail	20 cm.

The Sahara Desert, which acts as a great natural barrier to much of the fauna of Africa, is nevertheless the home of many species which have adapted themselves to the conditions of desert life.

One of these is the Fennec Fox (family *Canidae*), smallest and palest of the Foxes but with the biggest ears. It is one of five species of Fox found in Africa. This nocturnal carnivore spends the heat of the day in a scrupulously clean burrow which is lined with grass, hair and feathers. It feeds on birds and small rodents (for which it sometimes digs) and on insects such as locusts. Like many desert animals it can live for long periods without water. Its rapidity in digging is amazing. Litters consist of from two to five cubs.

The Jerboa is one of the animals upon which the Fennec lives. This is a member of the order *Rodentia,* of which there are also many species in Asia. All are expert jumpers, nocturnal desert dwellers who dig complex systems of burrows in which they form a community. Some plug the burrow entrance during the heat of the day. They exist almost entirely without water other than that which they obtain from the bulbs, roots and seeds which they eat. Three or four young are born at a time.

When travelling fast, Jerboas jump about three metres. Their long tails then serve as a balance or, when sitting upright, as a prop, forming a tripod with the feet.

Oryx (Gemsbok)	Length, head and body	250 cm.
(above)	Shoulder height	200 cm.
	Length of horns	100 cm.
Springbok *(below)*	Length, head and body	130 cm.
	Shoulder height	80 cm.
	Length of horns	35 cm.

The second great African desert, the Kalahari, has its own population of desert animals. One of these is the beautiful Gemsbok (family *Bovidae*) a race of the Oryx species which is found in varying forms through East and South Africa, and which is known as the Beisa.

Two other species are the almost white and very rare Arabian Oryx of the Arabian Peninsula, and the Scimitar-Horned Oryx of the Sahara. All produce a single calf at a birth.

The Oryx can scrape a living (often literally, as when digging for roots) from the most desolate country, and can subsist almost indefinitely without water. By its stamina and speed and by using its magnificent horns, it can defend itself against its principal enemies, the Lion and the Leopard.

The Springbok, the national emblem of South Africa, was once very numerous, migrating in gigantic herds across southern Africa in search of pasture. It is now very rare, protected in national parks and on farms in South Africa and Angola and in the Kalahari Desert. Its name derives from its habit of leaping when startled or at play, and standing high jumps of 3.5 metres are achieved.

Springbok have a curious fold of skin along the back. This is covered with pale hair which is erected into a tuft when the animal is frightened. Apart from this they are similar to Gazelles.

Single calves are born. Fortunately Springbok thrive and breed well in captivity, so may thereby be saved from possible extinction.

Sand Cat

Length, head and body	42 cm.
Length of tail	27 cm.

It is only a hundred years or so since the Sand Cat was first discovered in the Sahara Desert, and to this day little is known about it. What has become established is the fact that right across the desert areas of North Africa, through the Middle East and Persia and as far as the Transcaspian area of the Soviet Union, this species—or a race of it—is to be found.

The Sand Cat (family *Felidae*) is pale in colour, as desert animals tend to be. Its large ears, typical of a nocturnal animal which needs acute hearing for survival, are set very flat on the head. This feature can also be observed in other desert predators such as the Fennec Fox, apparently being necessary so that the animal can hide itself more easily when stalking its prey through vegetation or among rocks.

This beautiful little cat lives in holes and eats desert birds and rodents. It has coarse hair on the soles of its feet—another adaptation to desert life.

The other small cats of Africa include the Caracal (a species of Lynx) found in deserts in southern Africa, and the African Wild Cat, which lives in bush country and open forest and is very similar to the European Wild Cat. Another sizeable cat is the Golden Cat of the tropical forests, which is becoming very rare. Smaller species are the Jungle Cat, found in Egypt as well as in India, and the Black-footed Cat of the southern deserts.

INDEX

The Forest

Page 4 Galago : Potto

6 Mangabey : Colobus Monkey

8 Gorilla

10 Chimpanzee

12 Ruffed Lemur

14 Okapi : Duiker

16 Leopard

18 Serval

The Grasslands

Page 20 Anubis Baboon : Springhare

22 Lion : Lioness

24 Vervet Monkey : Cheetah

26 Spotted Hyaena : Black-backed Jackal

28 African Elephant

30 Brindled Gnu : Eland

32 Giraffe : White Rhinoceros

34 Impala : Thomson's Gazelle : Wart Hog

36 Hartebeest : Black Rhinoceros

38 Sable Antelope : Kudu : Zebra

40 Cape Buffalo : Hunting Dog

The Water

Page 42 Hippopotamus : Waterbuck

The Desert

Page 44 Arabian Camel

46 Fennec Fox : Jerboa

48 Oryx : Springbok

50 Sand Cat